MW00817182

MARLÈNE GRAVENBERCH

RE-EMBRACE YOU!

A Journey of Self Re-Discovery to Building Conscious Connections

Cover art by Ginoh Soerodimedjo

Dedication

To my beloved children, Saffira and Illio, and their wonderful spouses, Arseno and Veronique. To my grandchildren, who, along with their parents, are the light of my life and the source of my greatest joy.

To all my brothers and sisters, and to my cousins, who have always been more like siblings to me—your presence in my life is a gift.

To my strong aunty Carmen, who is like a mother to me. Your resilience and strength inspire me every day. You have faced so much and emerged stronger than ever, and for that, I am endlessly proud and grateful.

To my dear friends, Ginny and Sylvia, thank you for your unwavering support and for being the truest of friends.

To my sister from another mother, Chiquita, whose love and loyalty know no bounds—I am blessed to have you in my life.

To the father of my children, Tjark, to my in-laws, Martha and Arna, and your wonderful family, who still embrace me with open arms and hearts—I am truly thankful for you.

To my MAD2MAC (Make A Difference 2 Make A Change) empowerment sister support group, who have been my cheerleaders, my sounding board, and my constant source of encouragement.

To Ruth, Natalie, Susan, and Radjenie for your genuine curiosity about this book's journey.

And last but certainly not least, to all the women who are courageously taking the step to re-embrace themselves, welcoming themselves home to their true selves—this book is for you.

Table of Contents

Introduction

Welcome to
**Re-embrace You: A Journey of Self Re-Discovery to Build
Conscious Connections.**

Life has a way of throwing us off balance, making us question our worth
and purpose. I know this all too well, and I've walked a path of self-
discovery that was filled with ups and downs, heartaches, and triumphs.
I am not the only one who went through that path but also the different
clients who I have successfully coached the past four years. I discovered
the strength within me to heal and grow, as did my coaching clients.

This book is a reflection of my experiences and the wisdom I've gained
along the way. Throughout this book, you'll find stories, insights, and
exercises designed to help you reconnect with your true self. Through
relatable stories, practical advice, and thought-provoking exercises,
you'll learn how to heal past wounds, embrace your worth, and build
relationships that nourish your soul.

As you read, I encourage you to reflect on the areas where you want to
grow while being gentle with yourself. Take your time with the exercises
and let the lessons sink in. Remember, this is your journey, and it's okay
to move at your own pace. Use this book as your companion, allowing
it to inspire and support you as you navigate your own path.

Thank you for allowing me to be a part of your journey. I hope *Re-
embrace You* inspires you to embrace your true self and build the
conscious connections you've been longing for.

With love and heartfelt gratitude,
Marlène Gravenberch
Founder & Owner of Leadership Refocused

https://leadership-refocused.com/home
https://www.linkedin.com/in/marlene-gravenberch-5655a61a
https://www.facebook.com/LeadershipRefocused
https://www.facebook.com/MMIGravenberch
https://www.instagram.com/marlenegravenberch

Summary

Welcome to *Re-Embrace You*—your guide to finding yourself and personal growth. This book is all about *re-discovering* the real you and how this can greatly improve your relationships. In the first chapter, we'll look at the importance of self-awareness and understanding your core values. The introspective exercises provided will encourage you to contemplate deeply about what guides your life choices. Are you ready to begin your transformation? Let's get started!

In Chapters Two and Three, I explore the vital topics of identifying core values and establishing boundaries. You will get to do fun exercises that help you pinpoint your values and learn to set boundaries with my "Boundary Builder" tool, enhancing your overall well-being.

The following chapters go deeper into self-compassion and healthy relationships. Chapter Four shares my personal experiences with developing a positive relationship with myself, along with hands-on exercises for fostering self-love and acceptance. Chapter Five explores how these values play out in relationships through real-life scenarios and activities like "Planning Assertive Responses."

In Chapter Six, I dive deeper into the importance of boundaries in maintaining healthy relationships, with exercises like "Affirmation Creation" and "Reflective Action Plan" to emphasize the importance of establishing and respecting boundaries.

In the final three chapters, I delve into other crucial aspects that are also important to developing a healthy and fulfilling relationship with yourself, leading to a more fulfilling and balanced life. I further encourage you to keep reflecting and growing, showing how ongoing self-reflection helps build meaningful connections with yourself and others. The book wraps up with "Coming Home to Yourself," where we take a moment to reflect on our shared journey.

This book gives you hands-on advice for personal growth, focusing on the importance of values and boundaries to live a fulfilling life.

1. Introduction: Your Journey Begins Here

What if you woke up in a world where you honor your true self daily?

In the quiet dawn of a new day, you open your eyes to a world where the sun brushes the sky with its golden touch and paints it with hues of possibility. As you step into the day, you feel like a perfectly tailored suit—not conforming, but true to your individuality. Every move you make reflects your genuine desires, and every choice echoes with the beat of your heart.

Your colleagues can't help but notice how radiant you are, and your conversations go beyond the average, weaving beautiful patterns of real relationships. The office becomes your canvas, and your work is a masterpiece, full of joy and purpose. Under the warm rays of the sun, you free yourself from the constraints of social norms and fully immerse yourself in activities that align with your inner self.

As the day fades into a *peaceful* sunset, a deep sense of *satisfaction* envelopes you. You are amazed by the world you have helped shape, where honoring your true self has become a daily ritual. In this reality, authenticity is not just a virtue but the essence of your very being, woven into the rich fabric of a fulfilling life.

The transformative power of embracing yourself

We live in a world in which external expectations and societal standards often dictate the narrative of our lives. Despite that, numerous women are courageous enough to choose to go on that challenging yet powerful journey of true self-rediscovery and self-acceptance. This journey holds immense potential, not only for personal growth but also for fostering meaningful relationships.

Welcome to a world of empowerment, where embracing oneself is the key to a remarkable transformation. In the pages that follow, I will share and explore stories of myself and of courageous women and men who embraced their unique inner beauty. Their journeys of self-rediscovery have not only transformed their own lives but left a lasting impact on the meaningful relationships they form with others.

Meet Sara, a career-driven woman who has been navigating the corporate world for years. Societal norms have taught women like Sarah that if she wants to fit in in the corporate world, she has to conform to meet the high expectations and the rigid standards of success. While doing so, she was battling imposter syndrome and sacrificing her true self in pursuit of recognition in her profession.

However, as she delved into the depths of self-rediscovery, Sara realized that *re-embracing* her true self was the key to unlocking her full potential. As she *re-embraced* her self-confidence, it propelled her career to extraordinary heights and transformed her connections with coworkers. This led to a positive and collaborative atmosphere, igniting a strong sense of camaraderie within the workplace.

You will ask yourself: But how did Sara manage to rediscover her true self?

Re-discovering your true self: Exploring the essence of self-awareness and the role of core values

What does re-discovering yourself mean?

Rediscovering yourself is the process of understanding your true self: your values, your needs, and wants, even what food you like and dislike. Rediscovering yourself starts when you evaluate your life and think about what is energizing and what is not. What will bring more joy into your life? What inspires you to jump out of bed each morning?

According to scholars, self-rediscovery is a process of self-reflection, exploration, and growth. It involves gaining knowledge and understanding of your abilities, character, and feelings. It can also help you gain a clearer sense of purpose and direction in life. By rediscovering your true self, you empower yourself to trust your inner guidance and intuition. You no longer dismiss your heart's whispers as insignificant. Instead, you embrace them as beacons of truth, guiding you along a path that resonates with your soul's deepest yearnings.

How did Sara manage to rediscover her true self?

Below is a listing of how Sara started her journey.

1. **Initiation of reflection:**

   - Sara felt the need to transcend to a moment of solitude in her busy life.
   - In quiet spaces, she reflected on her life's journey and identified repetitive patterns.

Action: After a hectic work week, Sara spends quiet Sunday afternoons alone in a park, away from the noise and distractions.

2. Guidance from a coach

- Sara sought the help of a coach to guide her on her journey of self-rediscovery.
- The coach provided insights, tools, and support to facilitate her search.

Action: Sara hires a life coach who has regular sessions to help her explore her thoughts, set goals, and provide strategies for personal development.

3. Expression through writing:

- The coach encouraged Sara to put her thoughts on paper to express her emotions.
- This writing process allowed Sara to explore her innermost feelings and experiences.

Action: Sara buys a notebook and writes down her thoughts and emotions about her recent challenges at work and in personal relationships.

4. Questioning and examination:

- This process involved questioning her beliefs, examining past decisions, and identifying deeply resonating values.
- Sara's goal was to understand not only what she values but also why these values were important to her.

Discovery: Sara questions why she feels unfulfilled despite professional success and examines past decisions that led her to her current state. She discovered, for example, that making a career decision—in which she chose financial comfort over a more creative role that sparked her passion—has contributed to her current feelings of unfulfillment.

5. Questioning and examination

- Through reflection, Sara discovered and identified her core values, such as honesty, compassion, and creativity.

- These values became the guiding principles that defined her true identity.

Discovery: Through reflection, Sara identifies that honesty is crucial for her, valuing open communication and sincerity in all aspects of life.

6. Alignment of actions with values

- Sara committed to aligning her actions with her core values.
- This alignment helped Sara to create congruence between her core values and external choices and actions.

Discovery & Action: Sara, now recognizing her value of compassion, starts volunteering at a local community center to align her actions with her belief in helping others.

7. Challenges and growth:

- The journey was not without challenges, but letting go of old habits and embracing new ideas contributed to her transformation.

Discovery: Sara faces resistance when trying to expand her comfort zone, such as overcoming her fear of public speaking in order to pursue a passion.

8. Mindfulness practices:

- Being more self-aware became part of Sara's life; it became a way of living.
- Mindfulness practices like meditation and breathing became integral to her daily routine.

Action: Sara incorporates mindfulness by dedicating 10 minutes each morning to meditation, helping her stay present and centered throughout the day.

9. Understanding the continuous process:

- Sara realizes that self-rediscovery is an ongoing process.

- Each day presents an opportunity for her to delve deeper, refine her understanding, and embrace the unfolding path of self-discovery.

Discovery: Sara acknowledges that self-rediscovery is ongoing; each day, she reflects on her experiences, allowing room for personal growth and development.

Overall, Sara's journey involved introspection, guidance from a coach, and the discovery of core values, aligning actions with those values, facing challenges, and integrating mindfulness practices into her daily life.

2. Discovering Your Core Values

Embarking on a journey of rediscovery

As we embark on a journey to rediscover our own identity, it is important to go deeper into our core values. These values are our compass, pointing us toward truth and fulfillment.

In the hustle and bustle of everyday life, we are often caught up in the expectations and standards imposed on us by society. In the noise of outside influences, it's easy to lose sight of our own identity. But when we strip away the layers covered by society and get in touch with our core values, we begin to find ourselves.

Understanding core values

According to scholars, core values are the most fundamental set of beliefs and attitudes that guide the behavior of individuals and groups. Simply said: *Core values are the fundamental beliefs that guide our behavior, decisions, and interactions with the world.* They serve as the cornerstones of our identity, influencing the choices we make and the path we take in life. Recognizing and understanding these values is an important step in the journey to self-awareness.

THE "CORE VALUES EXPLORATION" EXERCISE:
AN INTERACTIVE EXERCISE TO HELP IDENTIFY YOUR PERSONAL
CORE VALUES

The objective of this exercise is to identify and prioritize your core values.

List 10 values that resonate with you (e.g., honesty, compassion, resilience)

Narrow down to your top 5 values and rank them in order of importance

Reflection: How do these values guide your decisions and behaviors?

List three moments when you felt truly aligned with your values.

For me, three moments when I truly felt aligned with my core values are:

1. Made the decision to communicate clearly about one of my core values, **'Fidelity,'** in an intimate relationship. When that was continually violated, I made the decision to step out of the relationship of almost 30 years.

2. Demonstrating another core value, **'Compassion,'** by choosing to go all the way bringing my brother and sister together through honest, intense, and challenging conversations,

listening to both with their own points of view and hurt feelings.

3. Choosing to offer free coaching sessions to women through the **nine**-month **Fempowerment** program I created, and to other individual women outside the program. This resulted in building the confidence and autonomy of these women to help them reach their full potential. This is fully aligned with another core value, **'Empowerment.'**

1.	
2.	
3.	

Living by your values brings personal fulfillment and alignment with yourself

Living by my values of Fidelity, Compassion, and Empowerment has brought me deep personal fulfillment and alignment with my inner self in various ways. Let's delve deeper into how each of these values contributes to my sense of fulfillment and alignment:

Fidelity

- **Personal Integrity:** Making decisions in alignment with the value of fidelity demonstrates a commitment to personal integrity. By communicating clearly and stepping out of a relationship when fidelity was continually violated, I honored my own principles and maintained authenticity in my actions.

- **Self-Respect:** Choosing to uphold fidelity in relationships reflects self-respect. It shows that I prioritize my own values and well-being, fostering a sense of self-worth and dignity.

Compassion

- **Connection with Others:** Demonstrating compassion by bringing my brother and sister together through honest and challenging conversations highlights the power of empathy and understanding. This connection with others enhances a sense of belonging and strengthens relationships, contributing to a fulfilling life.

- **Emotional Resilience:** Dealing with the passing of my brother after fostering compassion within the family demonstrates emotional resilience. Compassion allows me to navigate difficult situations with empathy and understanding, contributing to a deeper connection with myself and those around me.

Empowerment

- **Fulfillment through Contribution:** Offering free coaching sessions to women and creating the Fempowerment program aligns with my core value of empowerment. Contributing to the growth and autonomy of others brings a sense of fulfillment through meaningful impact and positive change.

- **Alignment with Purpose:** Supporting women to reach their full potential aligns with my values and purpose. This alignment enhances a sense of fulfillment as I actively contribute to the well-being and success of others, creating a positive impact on their lives.

In summary, living by these values brings personal fulfillment through self-respect, emotional resilience, meaningful connections, and a sense of purpose. Each moment described here reflects a conscious choice to align my actions with my core values, resulting in a more authentic and fulfilling life. This alignment contributes to a deeper understanding of self and a sense of purpose that extends beyond individual fulfillment to positively impact the lives of those around me.

Compromising your values

When we don't define our values clearly for ourselves and communicate them with others—or cannot withstand pressure from people around us with whom we have any type of relationship—we may land in a position in which we end up compromising our values. This can happen in various aspects of life, and the consequences can be profound.

Exercise 2: Reflect on a time when you had compromised your values

In the beginning of your journey, you will discover that it will surely be a challenge to let your values always lead the way.

That also happened to me. In the beginning of my journey, when I was just starting to identify my core values and develop that relationship with myself, I did not always have the courage to let my core values be my guide. Those were the times that I compromised my core values. Reflecting on those occasions, I want to share with you when two of my values became compromised:

Compassion

I discovered that an employee was going through a difficult time personally. At that time, I also had in the back of my head, *'There is always something going on with this employee.'* Despite being aware of the situation, and because I was biased, I failed to offer support, compromising my value of compassion.

Empowerment

As a first-time manager, I was hesitant to delegate tasks to other team members, fearing they might not be able to deliver what was required, but also fearing not being in control. This fear of losing control and authority hindered the empowerment of my team, as they were not given the opportunity to showcase their abilities.

In conclusion, this chapter underscores the transformative power of living in alignment with core values while acknowledging the challenges and potential pitfalls in maintaining this alignment that could result in compromising your values.

3. Setting Boundaries: Your Fortress of Self-Care

One of the most important parts of the self-care journey is setting healthy boundaries. These boundaries act as a fortress that protects your mental and emotional well-being. In this chapter, I will explore the concept of boundaries in more detail, along with its importance for self-esteem and self-care.

The essence of boundaries

Defining Boundaries

Understanding the importance of boundaries is essential to encouraging effective self-care. Boundaries are invisible lines that define your emotional, physical, and mental space for others. They act as a shield, protecting your identity and well-being.

Simplifying Healthy Boundaries

Contrary to misconceptions, setting healthy boundaries is not about building a wall that isolates you from the world. Instead, it's about creating a balanced and respectful environment in which you can thrive without compromising your authenticity. I will explore the differences between rigid, porous, and healthy boundaries, emphasizing the importance of the latter in self-care.

The role of boundaries in self-respect

Autonomy and Self-Respect

Boundaries are the cornerstone of freedom, and they allow you to assert your individuality and support your values. Let's talk about how setting and maintaining boundaries helps build self-esteem and empowers you to make choices that align with your authentic self.

Nurturing Relationships Through Boundaries

Healthy boundaries are not only crucial for your well-being, but they also play an important role in fostering healthy relationships. By being clear about your boundaries, you build a foundation of respect and understanding. This section will explore how boundaries can improve your communication with others.

Boundaries as pillars of self-care

Prioritizing Self-Care

Setting boundaries is an act of self-love and prioritizing yourself. This includes identifying your needs and ensuring they are met without guilt or compromise. We will explore practical ways to incorporate boundaries into your daily life, increasing your ability to engage in meaningful self-care practices.

Recognizing Warning Signs

Understanding when your boundaries have been tested or violated is essential to maintaining a strong fortress of self-preservation. This section will walk you through recognizing the warning signs and give you the tools to reinforce your boundaries when needed.

Practical exercises to establish and reinforce personal boundaries

Next, you'll find practical exercises to identify, define, and set boundaries. Complete the "Boundary Builder" exercise to define your boundaries.

Exercise 1: Boundary Builder

The Boundary Builder is a systematic and pragmatic way of defining and establishing personal boundaries in various social domains. The goal is to identify specific areas where boundaries need to be established, provide clear definitions for each, and measure the positive impact of respecting these boundaries. It empowers individuals to take control of their time, relationships, and personal space, promoting a more balanced and fulfilling life.

Identify areas where you need to set boundaries

The first step involves self-reflection to identify areas in your life where YOU find that you need to set boundaries. This may include but is not limited to:

a. <u>Work</u>: Define restrictions on work hours and acceptable out-of-hours work-related communications, and identify tasks beyond your responsibilities.

b. <u>Relationships</u>: Establish boundaries in personal relationships, such as preferred contact, personal space, and expectations for emotional support.

c. <u>Personal Time</u>: Recognize and communicate the need for personal time, hobbies, and self-care. Set limits on how you spend your free time and make sure it's in your best interest.

Defining clear and specific boundaries

Once YOU have identified the areas that require boundaries, the next step is to define them clearly and specifically. For example:

a. Work Boundaries:

- Set deadlines and be clear about when you are available for work-related tasks.

- Clearly communicate boundaries for answering work emails or out-of-work calls by appointment.

b. Relationship Boundaries:

- Clearly identify needs for personal space and alone time.
- Establish clear communication about expectations and boundaries in the relationship.

c. Personal Time Boundaries:

- Clearly define activities that contribute to your personal well-being, and devote dedicated time to them.
- Communicate these boundaries to others and make sure your personal time is understood and respected.

Reflection on well-being enhancement

Consider how honoring these boundaries contributes to your overall well-being.

a. Work-life balance: By establishing clear work boundaries, you can achieve a better work-life balance, prevent burnout, and promote mental and physical well-being.

b. Healthy relationships: Clearly defined relationship boundaries promote mutual understanding and respect, leading to healthy and satisfying relationships.

c. Self-care: Respecting personal time boundaries allows for better self-care and relaxation, improving mental health and overall well-being

Based on the provided guidelines and examples, define and establish two or three personal boundaries.

Instructions:

Identify two or three areas in your life where you feel that YOU need to set boundaries

Define clear and specific boundaries for each area identified

Reflection: How will honoring these boundaries enhance your well-being?

My own experience—how setting boundaries transformed my work-life balance

I have always been passionate about making a difference in the world. With a background in human resources and a strong sense of social responsibility, I found my calling working as an HR manager in various organizations. My job was demanding, with long hours, tight deadlines, and the emotional toll of working on projects that aimed to address pressing issues.

In the early years of my career, I found myself consistently overextending, often staying late at the office and sacrificing my personal time for the sake of my job. I believed that to make a significant impact, I needed to give my all, ignoring the toll it took on my mental and physical well-being. This relentless dedication led to me feeling as though I had no energy left in me, getting easily irritable, and affected my overall job performance and personal life.

One day, after a particularly challenging period that required me to work longer hours, while abroad visiting my little brother who was terminally ill, and with significant changes on the work floor, I realized that I needed to make a change for myself. I started to reflect on the importance of work-life balance and how I felt that I was not able to give any more as an HR manager. I felt there was nothing left in me. I began by setting clear boundaries between my professional and personal life, and then, after six months of careful consideration, I made the drastic decision to quit. I had to take time off for myself; I had nothing left to give.

I made it a point to prioritize self-care and took six weeks of vacation to recharge. Initially, some colleagues were surprised by my decision, finding me brave to choose for myself, because people thought that I had quit to take another job somewhere else. Since then (July 2023), I am committed to my newfound balance, doing what I am passionate about: business coaching with a significant emphasis on personal and professional development coaching, guiding individuals (also in the business environment) to be aware of keeping the work-life balance, among other things.

By initiating conversations about work-life balance within organizations, I advocate for flexible working arrangements, encouraging individuals—who are employees—to take breaks, and promoting a culture that prioritizes well-being.

With this newfound balance, I began to invest more time into my personal interests, like writing and spending more time with my family and intimate friends, fostering a healthier work-life dynamic. Finding this balance not only rejuvenated my passion for coaching but also enabled me to take courses to become a better coach.

Exercise 2: Identify one boundary you'll set this week and how it will benefit your well-being

Exercise 3: Self-Love Journal

Objective: Cultivate self-compassion and positive self-talk.

Instructions: If you are new to journaling, start with one week and every day, write down three things you appreciate about yourself. From there you can continue with two weeks, and this way you may want to make it a daily habit.

Begin each day, for the coming week, by jotting down three things you appreciate about yourself. These could be accomplishments, personal qualities, or moments where you showed resilience or kindness. Embrace the practice of acknowledging your own strengths.

_____

_____

_____

Self-criticism

Throughout the day, be aware of any self-critical thoughts that may arise. Instead of letting them linger, counteract them with compassionate and positive affirmations. Challenge your inner critic with self-loving statements.

Examples:

Self-criticism: "I should have done better in the presentation; I made too many mistakes."

Counter with compassion: "I may have made mistakes, but I also learned from them. I am human, and growth comes from embracing imperfections."

Self-criticism: "I don't deserve recognition for my work; it was just luck."

Counter with compassion: "I worked hard for my success, and I deserve to celebrate my achievements. Luck may play a role, but my effort and dedication are significant contributors."

Reflection: How does this practice influence your self-perception?

_____

_____

_____

_____

_____

When I do my self-reflection, I find myself more aware of my positive qualities and achievements. The act of countering self-criticism with affirmations creates a more compassionate inner dialogue with yourself. For me, as a result, I feel a greater sense of self-acceptance and a boost in my confidence. This practice has been a powerful tool for fostering my own positive self-perception.

This chapter provides detailed guidance on the dynamics of the power to set the boundaries for a more balanced and satisfying life. The combination of personal experiences, practical exercises, and insightful thinking adds depth and interactivity to the story, making it a valuable resource for those looking to improve their well-being going forward through effective boundary-setting practices.

4. Relationship with Self: Core Values as a Basis for Nurturing Self-compassion

When you are trying to figure out who you are and to become a better person, relationships with others are very important. This chapter talks about how identifying what is most important to you affects how kind you are to yourself. When you know and stick to what you truly value, it helps you treat yourself better. I will talk about the tough parts of being kind to yourself and share some tips for being nicer to yourself, accepting who you are, and thinking positively. This journey was not an easy one for me, and I'm still going through some struggles!

Defining core values

Core values are basically the deep beliefs that steer how you make decisions, act, and react in life. They are like a built-in compass, pointing you toward what really matters and making you feel fulfilled. Figuring out what these values are is super important for knowing who you are and living a life that's full of meaning. In the second chapter, I explained how you can find out what your core values are.

Impact of core values on self-compassion

When your actions align with your core values, it creates a great feeling, like everything fits perfectly. This feeling helps you be kinder to yourself as you figure out who you are, your authenticity, and how to accept yourself more and better. On the other hand, a lack of alignment with your core values can mess up how you feel inside, causing you to be hard on yourself and less happy. Here are some examples you might come across every day.

Alignment with your core values

Core Value	Action	Impact
Empowering and Elevating Others	Recognizing and praising my children, colleagues, and clients for their hard work, boosting their confidence and morale.	My children, colleagues, and clients will feel valued and are more likely to continue putting in effort, leading to a willingness to go the extra mile and personal fulfillment.
Knowledge and Wisdom Sharing	Sharing helpful tips or resources with a friend who is learning a new skill, contributing to their growth and development.	Sharing helpful resources with a friend accelerates their learning process and strengthens our relationship. By being open to sharing what I know and guiding others, I leave a lasting impression, steering toward more progress and success.

Misalignment with Core Values:

Core Value	Action	Impact
Empowering and Elevating Others	Taking credit for a team project's success that was largely due to the efforts of others, undermining their contributions and causing resentment.	Not giving the team the credit, they deserve creates resentment and distrust within the team. It undermines morale and teamwork, resulting in decreased productivity and a toxic work environment.
Knowledge and Wisdom Sharing	Not sharing what I know about key parts of a project or system with others.	This will slow down progress and stop us from growing personally and professionally. It will hold back everyone's ability to improve and to come up with new ideas.

The self-compassion journey

Understanding self-compassion

Self-compassion involves treating yourself with the same kindness and understanding that you would offer to a friend facing challenges. According to Dr. Kristin Neff, self-compassion just means making a U-turn, and giving yourself the compassion that you would naturally show toward a dear friend.

This dear friend is now *you*, who is struggling or feeling bad about yourself. It is now supporting *you* when you are facing a life challenge, feel like you are not doing the right thing, or you are making a mistake.

Instead of pretending everything's fine or carrying it with negative thoughts and feelings, you stop and say to yourself: ***"This is really hard right now, how can I comfort and care for myself in this moment?"***

The tips and techniques that I am about to share with you are the ones I practice myself on my own journey of self-compassion. My journey toward self-compassion was a transformative one. It reshaped my entire perspective on life. As a seasoned professional and personal development coach, I have always been great at helping others grow. But I, too, needed to go on a journey of my own. It was time for me to learn about self-compassion and self-love.

About three years ago, after a really tough coaching session, I felt a lot of self-doubt. The voice inside my head sounded a lot like the doubts my clients sometimes had, making me question if I was really good enough. It was in that moment of feeling vulnerable that I realized that I had to change how I saw myself.

I started to recognize my feelings without being hard on myself, the same techniques I used on my clients, and the way I often encouraged them in my coaching sessions. I encouraged myself to let myself feel uncomfortable and accept that making mistakes is just part of being human. It was at that moment that I realized there was a disconnect between what I was doing and what I truly believed in. This feeling of being disconnected made me feel even more troubled inside. That is how I started to use the techniques and exercises I will share next with you.

Techniques to cultivate self-compassion

1. Mindful self-compassion meditation:

- *Begin by finding a quiet space. Sit comfortably and focus on your breath.*

If, like me, you struggle with your mind wandering while meditating on self-compassion, it is important to gently direct your attention to the present moment without judgment. Here are some of the tools I use.

- **Breath as anchor**: Bring your attention back to the present moment. Focus on the sensation of your breath as it enters and leaves your body. Feel the air passing through your nostrils.
- **Labeling Thoughts**: Gently label the thought or distraction that pulled your attention away (*for example, silently say to yourself: "thinking," or "wandering," then gently guide your focus back to your breath*).
- **Compassionate Reminder**: Remind yourself that it's natural for the mind to wander and that you're not alone in experiencing distractions during meditation. Offer yourself words of kindness and encouragement (for example: "It is okay, just come back to the breath," or "I am gentle and patient with myself").
- **Visual Imagery**: Visualize yourself sitting in your favorite

place. Whenever your mind starts to wander, bring your focus back to this image and imagine yourself returning to a state of calm and relaxation.

- o *Acknowledge any feelings of discomfort or self-criticism.*
- o *Repeat affirmations such as "May I be kind to myself," fostering a gentle and supportive mindset.*

2. Positive affirmation journaling:

- Write down positive affirmations that resonate with your core values.
- Reflect on these affirmations regularly, reinforcing a positive and compassionate self-narrative. *Example: "I am worthy of (my) love! I accept myself just as I am."*

3. Values-based decision making:

- Use your core values as a compass for making decisions.
- Prioritize actions that align with these values, promoting your self-compassion. *Example: If one of your core values is connection, prioritize activities that nurture meaningful relationships.*

4. Self-reflection and mindfulness practices:

- Set aside time for regular self-reflection, examining thoughts and emotions without judgment. *It could be five minutes daily, marked in your calendar.*
- Integrate mindfulness practices, such as body scan meditations, to cultivate awareness and presence. Body scan meditations you can do any time of the day, scanning how you are feeling at that moment and why.
- If you can't find an answer yet, the answer will come at another moment. *Example: When facing a challenge, take a moment to observe your thoughts and respond with self-compassion. Say to yourself: "It's okay to not have the answer yet/now."*

Acceptance and positive self-talk

The Power of Acceptance: The foundation of self-compassion lies in accepting yourself, which involves acknowledging your shortcomings without judgment and enabling yourself to handle challenges by embracing yourself with all your strength and energy.

Cultivating positive self-talk

1. Identify negative patterns:

- Reflect on recurring negative self-talk patterns.
- Identify triggers and situations that activate these patterns.

Examples:

Negative pattern: Self-doubt, constantly questioning your abilities and worth.

Triggers: Comparing yourself to others, failure or setbacks, receiving negative feedback.

Challenge this negative thought with evidence. Replace self-critical thoughts with realistic and compassionate alternatives. *Example: Instead of "I always fail," shift to "I am learning and growing with each experience."*

If negative self-talk significantly impacts your daily life or mental well-being, consider seeking support from a coach, therapist, or counselor. They can provide personalized strategies and guidance to help you cultivate positive self-talk.

2. Gratitude practice:

- Cultivate a daily gratitude practice, focusing on positive aspects of yourself and your life. *Again, it could be five minutes daily, marked in your calendar.*

- Acknowledge achievements, no matter how small, reinforcing a positive self-image. *Example: Express gratitude for your strengths and resilience in challenging times.*

3. Compassionate self-affirmations:

I struggled with (imagined) imperfections like self-doubt, imposter syndrome, not feeling confident, and comparing myself to others. I turned them into compassionate self-affirmations and recognized that they make me unique.

I developed a list of compassionate self-affirmations. Here are some personalized affirmations I wrote down for myself and still use when I experience challenging moments. You, too, can write yours down, specific to your situation. Repeat your own compassionate self-affirmations regularly to boost your mood and confidence.

Compassionate self-affirmation against self-doubt:	Recognizing my uniqueness:
The times I am doubting myself I see them as chances to learn and find out more about who I am. They remind me that it's okay to make mistakes and that I can learn from them.	Dealing with self-doubt every day shows that I'm good at looking inside myself and figuring things out. It helps me stay humble and clear-headed in different situations. It makes it easier for me to connect with people on a real level.
Compassionate self-affirmation against imposter syndrome: I understand that it's normal to sometimes feel like I'm not good enough, but I choose to see these feelings as signs that I'm striving for growth and excellence. I'm not pretending to be someone I'm not; I've earned my achievements and opportunities like starting this journey, writing my solo book, conquering my fear to be more visible, meaning being afraid of putting myself out there and being seen. (name them).	**Recognizing my uniqueness:** When I feel like an imposter, it reminds me how dedicated I am to getting better and aiming high. It pushes me to work harder and shows me the value I bring to everything I do, thanks to my unique skills and perspective.

Compassionate self-affirmation against lack of confidence:	Recognizing my uniqueness:
I see moments of not feeling confident as chances to build my resilience and confidence. Every time I expand my comfort zone, I know I'm capable of overcoming challenges and growing stronger.	My journey to confidence shows my bravery and determination to push past my limits. It proves that I can thrive even when things get tough, making me someone who's adaptable and strong.
Compassionate self-affirmation against comparing myself to others: I let go of comparing myself to others and focus on my own journey and strengths. I celebrate others' successes while also being proud of my own progress.	**Recognizing my uniqueness:** When I compare myself to others, it reminds me of my empathy and understanding. It helps me appreciate everyone's unique experiences, making my relationships richer and more meaningful.

Learning to be kind to yourself by staying true to what really matters to you can completely change how you see yourself and how you feel. When we know what is truly important to us, and we treat ourselves with kindness, we start to feel better. This means being okay with who we are, being nice to ourselves even when things are not perfect, and encouraging ourselves with positive thoughts. It is not something that happens overnight; it is something we keep working on to become stronger, more resilient, and happier with who we are.

Exercise 1: Here are four activities to enhance self-love and acceptance.

1. Mirror affirmation exercise:

This exercise could make you feel very awkward when you do it for the first few times. I know I did, even though I live alone! But hang in there! To grow into this exercise, start with a mirror where you can only see your face.

- Find a quiet space with a mirror. If possible and you have a space for yourself, stand in front of a mirror.

- Look into your own eyes and say positive things about yourself out loud. You can use the compassionate self-affirmations you wrote down earlier, also recognizing your uniqueness.

2. **Love letter to yourself:**

- Set aside time to write a heartfelt letter to yourself, expressing love, gratitude, and acceptance.
- Include specific qualities you admire about yourself and acknowledge your achievements.
- Date the letter and keep it in a place where you can revisit it regularly.

This is a letter I wrote to myself, after a really long, long time, while writing this chapter. I needed to do this for myself again!

Paramaribo, March 29, 2024

To: My beloved Me, Marlène Gravenberch
From: Your beloved, long-lost friend

My dear beloved me,

I have been wanting to write to you for a long, long time, since it has been a while since I have written a letter to you. I just want to take a moment to let you know how much you mean to me. You are such an incredible person, and I am so grateful to have you in my life.

First off, I want to say thank you!

Thank you for all the hard work you put in every single day. Thank you for never giving up, even when things get tough. Your determination and resilience inspire me more than you'll ever know.

Thank you for every single step you've taken, every obstacle you've overcome, and every smile you've shared. You're a warrior, and your strength is nothing short of inspiring. You've got your fair share of scars and doubts. But that's what makes you!

It's also not just about what you do; it's about who you are.

You have such a kind and loving heart that shines through in everything you do. Your compassion for others is truly remarkable, and it makes the world a better place. Think about all the people you have coached, the people you have shown compassion and empathy to, the ones you have encouraged and listened to, without any judgment, who you have helped in every way possible, and made a difference in their life, knowingly and unknowingly.

You've got this unique calmness, this magic that makes people feel at ease, seen, loved, and know that they can trust you. Don't ever underestimate the power of your presence.

I also want to remind you to be kind to yourself. You are not perfect, and that's okay. You are human; humans aren't perfect, but they are amazing beings, with all their flaws, and so are you! And that is why you are also allowed to make mistakes.

Please remember this:

Give yourself grace and forgiveness, just as you would a friend. Another very important thing is, I want you to know that you are loved. You are worthy of love and being accepted just as you are, flaws and all. Not just by me alone, but by everyone lucky enough to know you.

You deserve to be your own best friend. Treat yourself with the same love and compassion you give to others. Forgive yourself for the mistakes, the slip-ups, and the wrong turns.

You are enough, exactly as you are in this moment. So don't you dare forget that! So, keep being your amazing self, and never forget how truly special you are!

With all my love and admiration,
Your beloved long-lost friend, Marlène

It is your turn now! Take a moment, grab a pen and paper, and write yourself a letter. Pour your heart out. Remind yourself of your worth, your strength, and your beauty. You might be surprised by what you find.

3. Body appreciation meditation:

Sit or lie down in a comfortable position. Close your eyes and focus on your breath to center yourself. Gradually shift your attention to different parts of your body, expressing gratitude and love for each.

Example: "I appreciate my strong legs that support me every day." You can do this with every part of your body.

4. Forgiveness meditation:

This exercise could also make you feel very awkward when you do it for the first time. It did make me feel awkward because we are not taught or used to forgiving ourselves. This forgiveness meditation I use for myself. With my coaching clients, I use forgiveness meditation that is specifically applicable to them alone. So is yours.

Find a quiet space and sit comfortably. Visualize yourself and slowly offer forgiveness for any perceived shortcomings or mistakes. Release guilt or resentment, allowing space for self-love and acceptance to flourish.

This is one I applied to myself.

I close my eyes and imagine myself standing right in front of me. It may seem awkward, but try it. I picture myself in the past, just from a different time in my life, also recent times. If you feel more comfortable picturing your younger version, use that image.

Now, I take a deep breath and look at that version of myself and I start talking like I am having a conversation with an old friend.

Hey, it's me. I know things haven't always been easy for us. I know sometimes you struggle with feeling confident. You look back at moments when you doubted yourself or felt like you weren't good enough. But you know what? It's okay. We all have those moments.

I forgive you for not always feeling confident. You're doing your best, and that's all that matters.

And how about comparing yourself to others? Yeah, I get it. It's hard not to scroll through social media and feel like everyone else has it all figured out. But let's not be hard on ourselves. Comparing ourselves to others doesn't do us any good.

I forgive you for those moments of comparison. You're on your own unique journey, and that's something to be proud of.

Now, let's talk about imposter syndrome. That's a tough one! Feeling like you're not qualified or deserving of success? Yeah, been there, done that. But guess what? You are qualified, and you are deserving.

I forgive you for doubting yourself. You're capable of amazing things, even if you don't always see it.

Okay, onto another biggie: being scared to put yourself out there as a coach. I totally understand. It's intimidating to step into that role and to share your knowledge and expertise with others. But you have so much to offer, and people need to hear what you have to say.

I forgive you for being scared. It's natural to feel that way. But don't let fear hold you back. You've got this!

And finally, let's talk about being more visible so people know what you're offering. It's tough to promote yourself, to shine a spotlight on your skills and services. But you know what? You have something valuable to offer the world.

I forgive you for holding back. It's time to step into the spotlight and show the world what you're made of.

From now on, I'm choosing to love and accept you just as you are. You're worthy of forgiveness, of kindness, and of all the good things life has to offer.

Feel that weight lifting off your shoulders as you say these words, feel that warmth of self-forgiveness filling you up from head to toe, like you would feel when forgiving someone really dear to you.

Take a moment to soak up this feeling of freedom and acceptance. When you're ready, open your eyes and carry this sense of peace with you wherever you go. You've just taken a big step toward healing and self-love. You got this!

Conclusion

Practicing these techniques and tools over time, you will begin feeling better about yourself. You will notice that you won't be so tough on yourself anymore. Instead, you will start treating yourself with kindness and empathy.

For me, this shift positively impacted my coaching. I became more compassionate, connecting with others on a deeper level. My change wasn't just internal; it reflected in my actions. Taking care of myself inspired others to find their own balance.

Being kinder to myself did not weaken my skills; it strengthened them and deepened my connections. My journey of self-compassion not only transformed my life but also continues to guide those I coach, showing them the power of kindness toward themselves.

5. Extending Values to Relationships

In the complexity of human relationships, sharing similar basic beliefs and ideas is what keeps them often strong. In this chapter, I will explore how our values influence how we interact with others. By figuring out how values play a role in relationships, we can see how being honest, empathetic, and collaborating on important things can truly make our connections with others better and stronger.

The foundation of core values

As mentioned in earlier chapters, inside each person, there are basic beliefs that are important to them. These beliefs guide how they make decisions and act. Think of them like a compass that shows the way in life. These beliefs affect what we choose and who we are. Before bringing these beliefs into relationships, it's important to know and talk about the ideas that drive our actions.

The evolution of personal values:

Values are not static; they change as we live, experience different things, and learn about ourselves. Understanding that our values can change helps us develop and improve while still holding onto the beliefs that really matter to us.

Core values in action

Living authentically: Living authentically means being true to yourself. When you act according to your beliefs and values, you show a genuine energy that draws others closer. Being real helps build trust and understanding in relationships.

Example: You're a vegetarian because you care about animal welfare. When you are invited to a barbecue, you politely decline meat dishes and explain your reasons. Your honesty about your values not only respects your own beliefs but also opens up a conversation in which others might learn about your perspective.

Mutual understanding and respect: Understanding and respecting each other happens when we bring our core values into our interactions. We create a space where differences are appreciated by expressing and respecting what matters to us. This respect sets the stage for positive connections.

Example: You and your close friend come from different cultural backgrounds. Instead of dismissing each other's customs, you take time to learn about and appreciate them. By celebrating each other's traditions, you create a living environment in which both of you feel understood and respected.

Empathy and compassion: Showing empathy and compassion comes from understanding the values that guide someone's actions. When we understand why others behave the way they do, we can relate to them better. This opens the door for caring connections where we acknowledge each person's unique journey.

Example: A friend is going through a tough time at work because they are being criticized for their ideas. Instead of judging them or offering quick solutions, you listen attentively and try to understand how they feel. By showing empathy and support, you help them feel less alone in their struggles.

Navigating conflicts with values: Dealing with conflicts is easier when we share values. Conflicts are chances to learn and grow, not roadblocks. When we stick to our shared principles, we can resolve conflicts gracefully.

Example: You and your partner have different spending habits. Instead of arguing over who is right, you sit down and discuss your financial values. You realize that you both value financial security but have different approaches. By focusing on your shared goal of security, you work together to create a budget that respects both perspectives.

Demonstrating values in relationships

Communication grounded in values: One of the best ways to show your values in your relationships is by how you communicate. When you speak or even just show how you feel through your actions, based on what you think is important, it helps create a place where people can be honest and open with each other. This section shows how being thoughtful in how you talk can make relationships stronger.

Example: Imagine you have a friend who always tells you the truth, even when it is hard. You know that when they talk to you, they mean what they say. It makes you feel safe and comfortable to share things with them because you know they won't lie to you or hide things. It is like having a friend who always tells you they love your cooking, but one day, they say they don't like it. You might feel a bit upset, but you know they are being honest. That honesty helps you trust them more.

Building trust through consistency: If you always stick to your values in everything you do, it helps others trust you more. When what you say matches what you do, it shows people that they can rely on you. This section looks at how being consistent can make trust grow and strengthen relationships.

Example: Think about a time when someone promised to help you with something, but they never showed up. You might start to doubt whether you can rely on them in the future. Now, imagine another friend who always keeps their promises. If they say they'll be there, they show up without fail. Over time, you start to trust them more because they're consistent. It is like when you have a favorite restaurant, and every time you go, the food tastes just as good as the last time. You trust that restaurant to always give you a great meal because they are consistent.

Cultivating positive influence: People who live by their values tend to inspire others in their relationships. The things they do and the way they live rub off on those around them. This section talks about how being true to yourself can make a positive difference to the people close to you.

Example: Have you ever had a friend who is always kind to others, even when they are having a bad day? Their positive attitude might rub off on you, and you find yourself being kinder to people, too. Or maybe you know someone who is really passionate about protecting the environment. They recycle, use reusable bags, and ride their bike instead of driving whenever they can. Seeing their dedication might inspire you to start making small changes in your own life to help the planet. That is the power of living your values - it can influence those around you in a positive way.

Creating a values-aligned community: Bringing your values into your relationships does not just affect the people you know. It can also shape the values of a whole group of people, like a community. This chapter explores how each person can help make a community where everyone shares the same important beliefs, and how that can make everyone's lives better.

Example: Picture a neighborhood where everyone cares about keeping the streets clean and safe. They organize regular clean-up days and look out for each other's homes. When someone new moves in, they are welcomed with open arms and encouraged to join in. Over time, this sense of community grows stronger, and everyone feels like they belong. It is like being part of a big family where everyone shares the same values and works together to make the neighborhood a better place to live.

Examples of how developing relationships based on your values can influence relationships.

I used two of my own core values to illustrate how you can develop a relationship based on core values.

Core value 1: Empower and elevate others

Developing a relationship based on this value:

1. Practice active listening

When talking to someone, make a conscious effort to really listen to what they are saying, without interrupting or thinking about what you will say next. Show interest in their thoughts and feelings by nodding, maintaining eye contact, and asking follow-up questions. This makes the other person feel valued and respected.

2. Offer genuine compliments

Take a moment to notice the strengths and qualities of the people around you, and sincerely compliment them on those traits. It could be something as simple as telling a friend that you admire their creativity or praising a coworker for their hard work on a project. Genuine compliments boost confidence and show that you appreciate and respect others.

3. Encourage and support

Cheer on the people in your life by offering encouragement and support when they need it. Celebrate their successes, no matter how big or small, and provide words of encouragement during challenging times. Letting others know that you believe in them can boost their confidence and strengthen your relationship with them.

Core value 2: Wisdom and knowledge sharing

Developing a relationship based on this value:

1. Share your knowledge and skills

If you have expertise or skills in a certain area, offer to share them with others. This could be teaching a friend how to cook a new recipe, helping a coworker learn a new software, or volunteering to tutor a classmate in a subject in which you excel. Sharing your knowledge and skills not only helps others grow but also strengthens your bond with them.

2. Be open to learning from others

Knowledge and wisdom sharing involves being open to learning from others. Approach every interaction with an open mind and a willingness to learn from others. Listen to different perspectives, ask questions, and seek opportunities to expand your knowledge and understanding. Everyone has something valuable to teach, and embracing this mindset can deepen your connections with others.

3. Express gratitude

Express gratitude for the opportunity to share wisdom and knowledge and also for having the opportunity to learn from others. Take time each day to reflect on the people in your life who gave you the space to share your wisdom and knowledge and who have made a positive impact on you, and express gratitude for their presence. Send a heartfelt thank-you note, give a warm hug, or simply say "I appreciate you" to let them know how much they mean to you. Gratitude fosters feelings of connection and strengthens relationships.

Exercise: Reflect on a recent interaction where your values positively guided your behavior.

Activity: Values reflection

Objective: Reflect on a recent interaction where your core values positively guided your behavior and explore the impact it had on yourself and others.

Instructions:

1. **Recall a recent interaction:** Think about a recent interaction you had with someone where you felt that your core values guided your behavior in a positive way. It could be a conversation with a friend, a decision you made at work, or an interaction with a stranger. If you have a hard time doing this exercise, take a look at the examples.

Your elderly neighbor was struggling with a heavy bag of groceries. Despite your rush to get home, you could not ignore her struggle. Kindness inside of you urged you to lend a hand.

2. **Identify your values:** Consider what values were important during this interaction. These could include honesty, kindness, integrity, empathy, respect, fairness, or any other values that are important to you.

Example: Core value is kindness

3. **Reflect on your behavior:** Reflect on how your values influenced your behavior during the interaction. Did you speak up for what

you believed in? Did you show empathy toward someone in need? Did you act with integrity even when it was difficult?

```

```

Explanation: Kindness influenced your behavior when you noticed that your elderly neighbor was struggling and you felt empathetic toward her situation. Instead of just walking past, you stopped to offer help because you could imagine how difficult it must be for her to carry those heavy bags with her arthritis acting up.

Kindness made you want to ease her burden and make her day a little easier. So, you put aside your own rush to get home and took the time to lend a hand, knowing it would mean a lot to her. It was like a little voice inside you was saying, "Hey, you can make a difference here." And seeing her smile and hearing her thank you showed you that kindness really does matter.

4. **Consider the outcome:** Think about the outcome of the interaction. How did your behavior impact the situation? Did it lead to a positive outcome for yourself, the other person, or both? Did it strengthen your relationship with the other person?

```

```

Outcome: The outcome of this interaction was overwhelmingly positive for both of you. It reaffirmed the importance of kindness in building meaningful connections and highlighted the joy that comes from helping others in need.

5. **Explore your feelings:** Reflect on how you felt during and after the interaction. Did acting in alignment with your values bring you a sense of fulfillment or satisfaction? Did it reinforce your commitment to living by your values?

```
```

Feelings: During the interaction you could have felt a mix of emotions. Maybe a bit rushed because you were trying to get home quickly. But as soon as you noticed her struggling, a feeling of empathy washed over you. You could not ignore her need for help, and that made you feel like you had to do something to make her day a little easier.

6. **Set intentions for future interactions:** Finally, think about how you can continue to let your values guide your behavior in future interactions. Set intentions for how you want to show up in your relationships and commitments moving forward.

```
```

Conclusion

Reflecting on interactions in which your values positively guided your behavior can help you gain insight into the importance of living authentically and with integrity. By acknowledging and honoring your values, you can cultivate meaningful connections and contribute to positive change in your relationships and communities.

As we conclude this exploration of extending core values to relationships, one big idea stands out: When we bring our core values into how we interact with others, it makes our lives richer and more colorful. Being true to ourselves, making an effort to understand each other, handling disagreements with care, and being a positive influence are not just things we do on our own; they are like threads that are woven together to make a strong and connected community.

By being mindful of our actions and sticking to our values, we each play a part in building strong and meaningful relationships. This helps create a world where being genuine, understanding each other, and sharing common values are the foundation of deep connections.

6. Healthy Relationships and Boundaries

Understanding how boundaries foster healthy connections and respect.

In today's world where technology and screens seem to be everywhere, it is easy to forget how important it is to connect with other people. Since the beginning of time, humans have depended on talking to each other, making friends, and being part of a community. In this chapter, I will talk about how these connections affect how happy we feel, how we get along with others, and even how our society works. I will start by looking at some research that experts have done to help us understand why human connection is so crucial for our well-being, our relationships, and the world we live in.

The neuroscience of connection

People are naturally social. We've always been this way, ever since we were babies. Back in the day, our ancestors stuck together to stay safe and find food. Dunbar (2010), who studied how humans have changed over time, says that being connected to others has always been extremely important.

He argued that understanding how our brains work when we connect with others can help us figure out ways to make people get along better and feel happier. This can be useful both for individuals and for society as a whole. For example, we can learn how to be more understanding and aware of others' feelings, and we can create rules and programs that encourage people to be more involved in their communities and help each other out.

Dunbar further argued that in today's world, we are often surrounded by technology but still feel lonely. It is important to remember how crucial it is to have friends and family. Knowing how our brains respond to human connection can remind us how much we need each other. By focusing on building strong relationships and staying connected, we can not only make ourselves happier but also make our communities and societies stronger (Dunbar, R. I. M., 2010).

According to Putman (2000), when people have strong social ties, it is not just good for them individually, but for everyone around them, too. Studies show places where people trust and help each other tend to have less crime, better schools, and more money for everyone. So, having good relationships is not just nice—it is good for everyone's health, happiness, and success.

Setting boundaries in healthy relationships

As people, we are naturally drawn to being with others. Relationships are like the spice of life—they make things richer, give us support, and make us feel fulfilled. Whether it is with family, friends, or a romantic partner, these connections bring a lot of joy. But, even with all that good stuff, we still need boundaries.

Think of boundaries in relationships like the lines on a road. They keep things moving smoothly and make sure everyone stays safe and is treated well. Without them, relationships can get messy, leading to fights or even hurting each other.

Now, why do we need these boundaries when we love being social? Well, consider this: Even if you are super close to someone, you are still your own person with your feelings and needs. Setting boundaries is not about shutting people out; it is about respecting ourselves and others. It is like saying, *"Hey, I care about you, but I also need to look after myself."* It is about finding that balance where both people feel heard and respected.

So, while we enjoy the company of others, it is important to remember that boundaries help us keep those connections strong and healthy. They are not about keeping people away but making sure everyone feels valued and safe. Setting healthy boundaries is one of the hardest things I experienced not only growing up but also as an adult.

The next sections in this chapter will provide information, guidance, tips, and tools to help you assess, set, and implement boundaries in various relationships.

Assess and implement boundaries in various relationships

Setting boundaries is super important for keeping our relationships healthy in all parts of our lives. Here are some relationships most of us have, with simple tips to start setting boundaries.

Work Relationships:

1. **Define work hours:** Set specific times for work-related activities and communicate them clearly to colleagues. Practice not responding to work emails or calls outside of these hours.
2. **Prioritize tasks:** Identify your priorities and learn to say no to tasks that do not align with your goals or workload capacity.
3. **Clarify responsibilities:** Clearly define your role and responsibilities within the team or organization to avoid overstepping boundaries or being taken advantage of.
4. **Limit access:** Keep personal information private and avoid discussing sensitive topics with coworkers to maintain a professional boundary.

Personal and Spousal Relationships:

1. **Daily check-ins:** Spend a few minutes each day discussing your feelings, needs, and boundaries with your spouse or partner. Talk about how you can support each other better.

2. **Respect alone time:** Communicate your need for alone time or personal space, and respect your partner's need for the same.

3. **Discuss expectations:** Have open discussions about expectations regarding household chores, finances, and decision-making to avoid misunderstandings.

4. **Practice active listening:** Listen attentively to your partner's concerns and boundaries without interrupting or dismissing them.

Parental Relationships:

1. **Set clear rules:** Establish clear rules and consequences for children's behavior, and consistently enforce them.

2. **Encourage independence:** Allow children to make age-appropriate decisions and respect their boundaries, such as privacy in their rooms or personal belongings.

3. **Lead by example:** Model healthy boundaries in your own behavior and interactions with others to teach children by example.

4. **Open communication:** Encourage open communication with your children, where they feel comfortable expressing their thoughts, feelings, and boundaries.

Friendships and Other Adult Relationships:

1. **Check-in regularly:** Schedule regular check-ins with friends to discuss any issues or concerns and ensure mutual understanding of boundaries.

2. **Respect differences:** Respect each other's differences in opinions, beliefs, and lifestyles without judgment or pressure to conform.

3. **Be assertive:** Practice assertive communication to express your needs, preferences, and boundaries clearly and respectfully.

4. **Limit toxic relationships:** Identify and distance yourself from

relationships with people who consistently disregard your boundaries or negatively impact your well-being.

Family Relationships:

1. **Family meetings:** Organize family meetings to discuss and establish boundaries that respect everyone's needs and preferences.
2. **Clarify roles:** Clarify roles and responsibilities within the family structure to avoid conflicts and misunderstandings.
3. **Respect individual choices:** Respect each family member's choices, lifestyles, and boundaries, even if they differ from your own. ·
4. **Manage expectations:** Communicate openly about expectations regarding family gatherings, financial support, and involvement in each other's lives.

My own experience navigating relationships with setting boundaries:

For years, from the early age of nine, I found myself shouldering the responsibilities of looking after siblings, cousins, and whoever else needed help. Saying no was nearly impossible for me. I was the go-to person for everything and everyone.

In my professional life, I felt it was my duty to take care of everyone's needs. I would lend a hand with tasks, automatically end up taking on responsibilities that were not mine, listen to everyone's problems, and feel the need to look for solutions. In my personal life, it was not much different.

As the years went by, I realized that this pattern was taking a toll on me. I was constantly exhausted, emotionally drained, and burdened with the weight of other people's troubles. It felt like I was carrying the world on my shoulders, and there was no end in sight.

Then, about two and a half years ago, something clicked inside me. I could not keep living like this. I knew I had to change, but breaking out of the cycle of constantly doing too much was not easy. It took time and effort to recognize that setting boundaries was not selfish—it was necessary for my own well-being.

I started small, learning to say no to minor requests and gradually working up to more significant ones. It wasn't easy at first, and some folks who were used to me always saying yes didn't like it when I started saying no.

But I kept at it, practicing and staying determined. Eventually, I got better at speaking up for myself and letting people know my boundaries in a clear and firm way. Every time I set a boundary, there was pushback—from others and even from my own doubts and worries.

I felt guilty, and fearful thoughts crept in, making me question if I was being selfish or letting people down. But I refused to let those voices dictate my worth. I knew that honoring my own needs was the ultimate act of self-respect—a necessary step on the path to true fulfillment.

I found some helpful tools along the way. First off, I started thinking about what I really needed and what I could let go of. If something was too much for me, I learned to say no or pass it on to someone else. Writing down my thoughts and feelings helped a lot, too. It let me see what was stressing me out and why.

Checking in with myself regularly about my boundaries was key. It helped me handle the tricky emotions that popped up when I set boundaries. Setting clear goals helped me stick to what mattered most to me, even when others tried to work that guilt into me, steer me in a different direction, or push me around.

It's been about two and a half years since I began this journey, and let me tell you, things have really changed for me. I feel so much more at peace and free now. Saying no does not make me feel guilty like it used to. I have realized that looking out for myself is important too. I get to decide where I want to spend my time and energy. I do not have to carry everyone else's burdens on my shoulders anymore.

Today, I feel confident in my ability to set healthy boundaries, both in my professional and personal life. It has been a journey with ups and downs, but I am thankful for how much I have grown. Most importantly, I have learned that looking after myself is **not selfish—it is necessary**.

To anyone feeling overwhelmed by others' demands, I encourage you to take that initial step toward regaining control of your life. You deserve love, respect, and happiness, and it begins with respecting your own boundaries. You have the power to rewrite your story and create a life that honors your truest self.

Exercises, tips, and tools to assess and set boundaries

Relationship Boundary Assessment

Objective: Evaluate and adjust boundaries in relationships

Instructions:

1. **Identify key relationships:**

   - List the significant relationships in your life, such as family, friends, and colleagues. You can also be more specific and list your spouse, children, and parents.
   - Consider the dynamics and expectations within each relationship.

Just to give you an idea: Dynamics in a family relationship could be all about love, support, understanding, and an unspoken agreement that you will always be there for each other, no matter what. You know each other well enough that you can sense when something is off or when someone needs space. But at the same time, you are pretty open about your feelings and thoughts toward each other. There is a sense of trust that allows you to be vulnerable with each other.

2. **Reflect on current boundaries:**

    - Assess the existing boundaries in each relationship.
    - Note areas where boundaries are clear, where they might be too rigid, or where they might be lacking.

_____

_____

_____

_____

3. **Evaluate emotional boundaries:**

    - Think about how you feel in the relationships you listed.
    - Identify instances where emotional boundaries may be blurred or where you might be overly invested.

_____

_____

_____

_____

4. **Assess time and availability:**

    - Reflect on how you allocate your time in various relationships.

- Consider whether there are instances where your availability might need adjustment for a healthier balance.

_____

_____

_____

_____

5. Communication boundaries:

- Evaluate how effectively you communicate your needs and expectations.
- Identify areas where improved communication could contribute to healthier boundaries.

_____

_____

_____

_____

6. Recognize personal needs:

- Consider your own needs and well-being within each relationship.
- Reflect on whether you have been prioritizing self-care and personal space.

_____

_____

_____

_____

How can clearer boundaries positively impact these relationships?

Making sure everyone knows and respects the rules in relationships is very important for making them work better and making everyone feel good. This is why:

1. **Improved communication:**

   - Clear boundaries facilitate open and honest communication.
   - By expressing needs and expectations, misunderstandings can be minimized, fostering a deeper understanding between individuals.

2. **Respect and understanding:**

   - Well-defined boundaries contribute to mutual respect.
   - When boundaries are respected, it creates a foundation of trust and understanding, improving the relationship between two people.

3. **Balanced reciprocity:**

   - Clear boundaries help establish a balanced give-and-take in relationships.
   - Ensures that neither party feels overwhelmed or neglected, leading to a more equitable and fulfilling connection.

4. **Emotional well-being:**

   - Setting healthy emotional boundaries helps you to avoid feeling drained or overwhelmed by emotions.
   - Understanding and honoring your emotional boundaries leads to better, more balanced interactions with others.

5. **Personal growth:**

- Establishing boundaries allows room for personal growth and individual pursuits.
- Each person can thrive independently, contributing positively to the relationship through their evolving strengths.

6. **Reduced resentment:**

- Clear boundaries prevent the build-up of resentment.
- By addressing and adjusting boundaries as needed, potential sources of resentment can be proactively managed and resolved.

Affirmation Creation

Objective: Reinforce commitment to personal boundaries.

Instructions:

- Create three affirmations that reinforce your dedication to honoring boundaries.
- Repeat these affirmations daily for a week.

These are my own:

1) I prioritize respecting boundaries. 2) I honor my own and others' limits. 3) Boundaries are essential for healthy relationships.

Reflect on how your own affirmations impact your mindset and behavior:

_____

_____

Planning Assertive Responses

Objective: Develop assertive yet respectful responses to boundary violations.

Set your boundaries according to your core values. If a core value is about spending time with your family, then you will set a firm boundary about working late. Boundaries are set by you and that makes them yours. Lots of your boundaries may be aligned with those of people close to you, but some will be specific to you. It is important to have your boundaries clear before entering any situation. In this way, you will be less likely to end up doing something that does not sit right with you, and you will know how to say no.

How to say NO

You have the right to say no! But how to say it is always the question. Here are some phrases you can use that have helped me too.

I can't agree with this.	I don't like this.	I'm unable to help you with that.
I won't go any further than ___.	Could you please stop?	This doesn't suit me.
I'd rather not do that.	Not right now.	I've made up my mind not to.

Support what you say by doing the following:

Show respect	Be ready upfront
Don't shout, insult, or ignore people. It is fine to be assertive, but people will understand you better if you are polite.	Consider what you want to say and how you will say it before diving into a tough conversation. Doing this can boost your confidence in what you are about to say.
Give-and-take	**Be confident in your body language**
When appropriate, listen and consider	Face the other person, make eye

the needs of the other person. You never have to compromise, but give-and-take is also part of any healthy relationship.	contact, and use a steady tone of voice at an appropriate volume (not too quiet, but not too loud).

Practice!

What if you were in these situations?

1. Your sister asks you to babysit your four-year-old niece on a Sunday evening and you already have other plans. *How will you respond?*

_____

_____

2. You were absent for a week from work because of a medical condition. On your first day back, a colleague asks why you were not at work. Since this is very personal, you do not want to share this information. *How will you respond?*

_____

_____

3. Your friend calls you during dinner with your family you have not seen in a long time. She is very upset and wants to talk to you. You want to get back to dinner with your family. *How will you respond?*

_____

_____

Conclusion

Taking the time and effort to figure out and adjust boundaries in your relationships is important. It helps to build a strong foundation of mutual respect, understanding, and support. As you work through these changes, keep in mind that having good boundaries is good for both party's happiness and health.

7. Deeper Dive into an Intimate Relationship with Yourself

Now that we have gone in-depth in the fundamentals of what are the important aspects to start building a relationship with yourself and others, in this chapter I will dive into other aspects that are also important to developing a healthy and fulfilling relationship with yourself, leading to a more fulfilling and balanced life. I will also share with you my own experience and cases of individuals I have coached. The names of all individuals have changed for their privacy.

In the following paragraphs, I will highlight three aspects that are also important in the journey of developing a relationship with yourself.

The first aspect is:

Self-awareness!

Self-awareness is like having a mental mirror that lets you see your thoughts, feelings, and behaviors. It is about understanding what makes you tick, what triggers your emotions, and why you act the way you do. This knowledge helps you navigate life with more intention and less reactivity.

Imagine you are on a road trip without a map or GPS. You might end up lost, frustrated, and going in circles. Self-awareness acts like that map or GPS, guiding you through the twists and turns of life. When you are self-aware, you can recognize when you are feeling stressed, understand why, and choose healthier ways to cope rather than just reacting impulsively.

Here are a few key reasons why self-awareness is crucial for a healthy and fulfilling relationship with yourself:

1. *Better decision-making*: When you understand your values, strengths, and areas that need further development, you make choices that align with who you truly are. This leads to a more satisfying life because you are living authentically. More about <u>authenticity</u> is further in this chapter.

Case 1:

Below is a case of Henry (the name is changed to protect the coachee) to stress how self-awareness guides better decision-making.

Henry is a marketing professional. He has spent time reflecting on his values and realizes that creativity, family, and personal growth are most important to him. He also knows his strengths include problem-solving and communication, but he recognizes he needs to develop his technical skills in digital marketing.

One day, Henri is offered two job opportunities:

- A high-paying corporate role that requires extensive travel and focuses on traditional marketing strategies.
- A slightly lower-paying position at a local startup that emphasizes creative digital marketing projects and allows flexible work hours.

During the coaching sessions, we did the *"Core Values Exercise"* and Henri learned to understand his values better, so Henry made a decision based here upon. Henry values family time and creativity, which aligns more with the startup role that offers flexibility and creative projects. Additionally, this role will help him develop his digital marketing skills, aligning with his goal of personal growth.

So, Henry chose the startup position, and as a result, he feels more fulfilled and authentic in his work because it aligns with his values and supports his strengths and development areas. This leads to a more satisfying professional and personal life.

2. *Improved relationships*: Knowing yourself helps you communicate better and set healthy boundaries. You can express your needs and understand others' needs more clearly, leading to stronger and more meaningful relationships.

Case 2:

This case is a personal experience from one of my former workplaces. I often felt overwhelmed and stressed when a colleague, Alex (changed the name to protect the person), assigned last-minute tasks. Reflecting on this, I recognize that I am a person who prefers having clear plans and advance notice to manage my workload effectively.

Understanding this about myself, I decided to have a conversation with Alex. I explained that while I appreciate the collaborative nature of our work, I work best when I have more lead time to prepare for tasks. I expressed this calmly and suggested setting up regular meetings to discuss upcoming deadlines and tasks in advance.

The tone and respect I expressed, also helped me in Alex listening and realizing that he can be more organized in his task assignments. He agreed to the regular meetings and started giving me more notice. I, in turn, felt less stressed and more in control of my workload.

As a result, the quality of my work improved, and I felt more satisfied with my job. The mutual understanding and improved communication enhanced our working relationship, making team projects more efficient and enjoyable for both of us.

3. *Enhanced emotional regulation*: By recognizing your emotional triggers, you can manage your reactions more effectively. This means less stress and fewer regrets over impulsive actions.

Case 3:

This case is also a personal experience. I must confess, I had to work hard on this one and now I can share that for a few years, I can regulate my emotions in traffic. Before, when I got stuck in traffic, and someone cut me off abruptly, normally, this would make me feel angry and stressed, and I reacted by honking my horn, yelling, and even making rude gestures. Now that I have been working on recognizing my emotional triggers and knowing that aggressive driving is one of them, I take a deep breath (sometimes just shake my head), reminding myself that getting angry won't help the situation. Now, I focus on staying calm because I also have my favorite music on and singing along.

As a result, I am in a better mood in traffic, with less stress, and without regretting any impulsive reactions. This not only improves my mood but also contributes to me experiencing my day as more pleasant, more positive, and more productive.

4. *Increased Self-Acceptance*: Self-awareness fosters self-acceptance. You become more forgiving of your flaws and celebrate your strengths, leading to a healthier self-image and greater self-confidence.

Case 4:

During the period of coaching, Jane (the name is changed to protect the person), was taking piano lessons. At first, she felt frustrated because she made lots of mistakes and compared herself constantly to the others in her class, who seemed more skilled. During the coaching sessions, we went through some specific exercises to guide Jane to focus on her self-awareness. She started to pay attention to her thoughts and feelings, recognizing that everyone has their own learning curve.

Through this self-awareness, Jane started to acknowledge her progress, no matter how small. She realized that making mistakes is a natural part of learning. Jane became more accepting of her imperfections, understanding that they don't define her abilities or worth. She started to celebrate her small victories, like mastering a difficult piece or improving her timing.

As a result, Jane's self-acceptance grew. She became more forgiving of her flaws and less critical of herself. Her healthier self-image and increased self-confidence motivated her to keep practicing and enjoying her piano journey.

5. *Growth and development*: Being aware of areas where you want to improve allows you to set realistic goals and work towards them. This continuous self-improvement contributes to personal growth and a sense of accomplishment.

Case 5:

A coaching client, who was aware of her challenges related to assertiveness; difficulty managing new situations over which she has no control; feeling overwhelmed by her tendency to give too much; finding the balance between work, personal life, and self-care; taking critical feedback very personally; doubting her abilities in the face of setbacks; responding to stress primarily by going into "fight mode", which can result in explosive reactions.

These patterns in some ways were hindering her in achieving a healthy balance and effectively coping with challenging situations. By the end of the fourth session (we had bi-weekly sessions), we both (the coaching client and I) identified a completely different attitude that confirmed all the below-mentioned observations about her.

- Talking helps
- Has better control over different kinds of challenges
- Identifies better now what SHE needs
- Experience more structure in her thought patterns
- Feels less overwhelmed

- Experience that there are multiple solutions
- No longer feels being the victim
- Taking the initiative to do something fun with friends
- Realizes that she does not have to solve everything
- Sees HERSELF through HER own eyes
- Being an entrepreneur, she gained much more self-confidence, which made her trust herself more. She also trusts her own knowledge more.
- The core value exercise has also helped her with establishing the aforementioned
- She also learned to do a lot of self-reflection!

This continuous self-improvement contributes to the client's personal growth and a sense of accomplishment in her professional life.

Techniques for enhancing self-awareness

To cultivate self-awareness, you can try:

- **Reflection**: Spend time thinking about your day, your actions, and your feelings. Journaling can be a helpful tool for this.
- **Mindfulness**: Practice being present in the moment. Pay attention to your thoughts and feelings without judgment.
- **Feedback**: Seek feedback from trusted friends or mentors. They can provide insights into your behavior that you might not notice.
- **Therapy or coaching**: Professional guidance can help you uncover deeper aspects of yourself and develop greater self-awareness.

The <u>second</u> aspect is:

Self-respect

Self-respect means valuing yourself and treating yourself with kindness and consideration. It is about recognizing your worth and standing up for your own needs and rights. When you have self-respect, you believe that you deserve to be treated well by yourself and others. Having self-respect plays a crucial role in building a healthy and fulfilling relationship with yourself.

Developing self-respect involves a few key practices. I want to dive deeper into two of them:

- setting personal standards and holding yourself accountable
- recognizing and celebrating personal achievements

Setting personal standards

These are the guidelines you set for how you want to live your life and treat yourself. These standards help you decide what is important to you and how you expect to be treated, guided by the following:

1. **Identify your values**: Think about what matters most to you. Is it honesty, kindness, hard work, or something else? Your values will shape your standards if needed.
2. **Set clear boundaries**: Decide what behaviors are acceptable and unacceptable from yourself and others. For example, you might decide that you won't tolerate being spoken to disrespectfully.
3. **Write them down**: Putting your standards in writing can make them feel more concrete and help you remember them.

Regarding values and boundaries, I have talked about this in the first six chapters extensively. Please go back to the exercises, if needed.

Holding Yourself Accountable

Accountability means making sure you stick to your personal standards. It is about being honest with yourself and following through on your commitments, guided by the following:

1. **Self-reflection**: Regularly check in with yourself to see if you are living up to your standards. *Ask yourself, "Am I acting in ways that align with my values?"*
2. **Set goals**: Create specific, achievable goals that reflect your standards. *For example, if one of your standards is to be healthy, set a goal to exercise three times a week.*
3. **Track progress**: Keep a journal or use an app to track your progress. *Note where you are doing well and where you might need to improve.*
4. **Adjust when needed**: Sometimes life changes, and your standards might need to evolve. *It is okay to adjust them to better fit your current situation and priorities.*

Recognizing achievements:

Taking time to acknowledge your accomplishments, no matter how small, helps build self-respect.

1. **Make a list**: Keep a list of your achievements, big and small. *This can include finishing a project at work, sticking to a workout routine, or even just getting through a tough day.*
2. **Reflect regularly**: Set aside time each week or month to review your list. *Reflect on what you have accomplished and how it makes you feel.*

Celebrating Achievements:

Celebrating your achievements reinforces your sense of self-worth and motivates you to keep striving.

1. **Reward yourself**: Treat yourself when you reach a goal. This does not have to be extravagant. *It could be a nice meal, a day off, or a fun activity you enjoy.*
2. **Share with others**: Tell a friend or family member about your accomplishments. *Sharing your successes with supportive people can make the celebration even sweeter.*
3. **Create traditions**: Develop personal traditions for celebrating your achievements. *For example, you might treat yourself to a favorite dessert whenever you complete a big project.*

When you are setting personal standards and holding yourself accountable, you create a framework for living a life that aligns with your values.

Recognizing and celebrating your achievements reinforces your self-worth and encourages you to continue growing.

Together, these practices help you develop strong self-respect, leading to a more fulfilling and balanced life.

The <u>third</u> aspect is:

Authenticity

I have mentioned earlier two essential aspects of developing a healthy and fulfilling relationship with yourself and living a balanced and meaningful life. The third key aspect is *authenticity*. I am going to break down what it means to be authentic and how it can positively impact your life by looking at two important components: *being true to yourself* and *embracing vulnerability*.

Be True to Yourself by:

- *Living authentically*: Living authentically means being true to who you really are. This involves expressing your true thoughts, feelings, and desires, rather than hiding them or changing them to fit in with what others expect of you. This is not an easy one, but in the process of developing a relationship with yourself, this is crucial! *If you can't be true to yourself, who will?* When you live authentically, you make choices that align with your core values and beliefs, even if they are different from what others think you should do.

Here is an example where it is not easy to choose to live authentically.

At the office where the majority of your colleagues spend their lunch breaks gossiping about others and discussing topics you find uncomfortable. Despite this, you usually join them because you don't want to seem rude or be left out. Living authentically would mean that you would choose to spend your lunch breaks differently. So, instead of joining the gossip sessions, you start bringing a book you have been wanting to read or you go for a walk to clear your mind and enjoy some fresh air.

Colleagues will probably question why you are not joining them, and you will probably feel a bit awkward. However, by sticking to your decision, you are honoring your true self and what is important to you. Over time, you will notice that you feel more energized and content because you are spending your breaks in a way that aligns with your values.

Additionally, in the future, this change may have a positive ripple effect. Perhaps a colleague who also dislikes gossip but feels pressured to fit in sees your example and joins you for a walk or starts their own quiet activity. By living authentically, you not only enhance your own well-being but also potentially inspire others to do the same.

- *Avoiding conformity*: It is common to feel pressure to conform to others' expectations, whether from family, friends, or society. However, constantly trying to meet others' expectations can lead to dissatisfaction and a loss of self-identity. Instead, focus on what truly makes you happy and fulfilled.

<u>I will share my own story with you here.</u>

Ever since I was a little girl of 7–8, I knew I wanted to become a teacher, but my father wanted me to become a physician. I decided (I was already 17–18) to drop out of college, and go to college to get my degree to become a teacher. I am so glad and proud of myself that I made the choice to follow my heart, even when it was a difficult decision to make. Looking back, it brought and still brings me so much satisfaction. My career started with teaching where I educated and empowered children, later in my career the group consisted of young adults, and now the group is a mix of workforce, entrepreneurs, CEOs, and individuals who need coaching.

- ***Maintaining integrity:*** Being true to yourself also means maintaining your integrity. This involves being honest with yourself about who you are and what you want. It means not compromising your values or pretending to be someone you are not just to gain approval from others. Integrity builds self-respect and confidence, which are crucial for a healthy relationship with yourself.

<u>Below is an example of how to maintain integrity.</u>

In the company where you work, most of your colleagues frequently stay late to complete their tasks, even though this means compromising their personal time and well-being. The culture in your office subtly implies that staying late is a sign of dedication and commitment, and those who leave on time are often seen as less committed.

But *you value work-life balance and believe that it is important to leave work on time to spend quality time with your family, pursue personal interests, or simply rest. You have been able to complete your tasks efficiently within regular working hours and don't see a need to stay late just to fit in.*

- *You recognize that maintaining a balance between work and personal life is crucial for your overall well-being and productivity.*

You are aware that staying late at work goes against your values and priorities.

- *You acknowledge your feelings and admit that the pressure to stay late makes you uncomfortable. You are honest with yourself about your need to uphold your work-life balance, even if it means being different from your colleagues.*

- *When asked by your manager or colleagues why you don't stay late, you explain that you prioritize efficiency during regular hours and that maintaining a healthy work-life balance is important to you. You express this calmly and confidently without feeling guilty or defensive.*

- *Despite any subtle pressure or judgment from others, you continue to leave on time, demonstrating your commitment to your values. You resist the urge to stay late just to gain approval or fit in with the office culture.*

- *By staying true to your principles, you build self-respect and confidence. You know that you are living in alignment with your values, which strengthens your sense of integrity. Over time, this consistency in your actions helps you develop a healthier and more fulfilling relationship with yourself.*

Your colleagues may initially be surprised or even skeptical of your decision, but over time, they might start respecting your commitment to your values. Some may even be inspired by your example to rethink their own work habits. Most importantly, you feel more authentic and content because you are living in a way that truly reflects who you are and what you believe in.

Practical steps to authenticity

1. **Self-reflection:** Spend time regularly reflecting on your thoughts, feelings, and actions. Journaling can be a helpful tool for this. *Ask yourself questions like, "What do I truly want?" and "Am I living in a way that aligns with my values?"*

2. **Set boundaries:** Learn to say no to things that don't serve your well-being. *Setting boundaries helps you protect your time and energy, allowing you to focus on what truly matters to you.*

3. **Practice self-compassion:** Be kind to yourself. Accept that you are human and that it is okay to have flaws and make mistakes. *Treat yourself with the same compassion you would offer a friend.*

4. **Seek support:** Surround yourself with people who support and encourage your authentic self. *Avoid those who pressure you to conform to their expectations.*

5. **Take small steps:** Start with small acts of authenticity. *Express your opinions honestly in conversations, and gradually make choices that reflect your true self.*

Living authentically helps you to create authentic connections. When you are open and honest with yourself, it also improves your relationships with others. People are more likely to connect with you on a deeper level when you show your true self.

Last but not least, the <u>fourth</u> aspect:

Vulnerability

In the journey of building a healthy and fulfilling relationship with oneself, embracing vulnerability is also a fundamental step. Often, the word "vulnerability" is associated with weakness or the risk of being hurt. However, in the context of developing a relationship with yourself, vulnerability is not about weakness. It is about having the courage to face your emotions, fears, desires, and uncertainties head-on, without self-judgment. Vulnerability means being open and honest about your feelings, thoughts, and experiences, even if it means you might get hurt, judged, or rejected.

Whether you're working on understanding yourself better or building stronger relationships with others, being vulnerable is key. It helps build trust, create closer bonds with people, and helps you grow as a person.

The power of vulnerability

Being vulnerable might sound simple, but it requires a deep dive into your own thoughts and emotions. It means sitting with your feelings, even the uncomfortable ones, and not rushing to brush them off. This can lead you to understand your core values, what truly motivates you, and, importantly, what you might need to change in your life.

Acknowledging your flaws

Part of being vulnerable with yourself is recognizing your flaws. Everyone has them; it is a natural part of being human. Instead of hiding these flaws or being overly critical about them, acknowledge them with kindness and patience. This acceptance does not mean resignation but rather an understanding that personal growth is a continuous process.

Listening to your inner voice

Often, we are our harshest critics. Learning to listen to your inner voice with empathy and compassion can significantly change how you relate to yourself. When you make a mistake, instead of beating yourself up, try to offer words of encouragement that you would typically reserve for a friend. This nurturing approach fosters resilience and a more positive self-view.

Facing your fears

Vulnerability also involves facing your fears. Whether it is the fear of failure, rejection, or not meeting expectations, confronting these fears is crucial. It is about asking yourself tough questions: *Why does this fear exist*? *Is it holding me back*? Often, just the act of facing these fears can reduce their control over you and lead to breakthroughs in personal development.

The joy of genuine self-expression

Lastly, vulnerability allows for genuine self-expression. This means celebrating your successes and sharing your passions without fear of judgment. It means being honest about your aspirations and the things that delight you, regardless of how others might perceive them.

By embracing vulnerability, you create a space where you can be truly honest with yourself, which is the cornerstone of any healthy relationship. This will set the tone for how you interact with others and how you face the world, equipped not just with self-acceptance but also with the confidence that comes from truly knowing and respecting yourself.

8. Reflection and Next Steps

As you turn to one of the last chapters in this journey, this chapter is all about reflection. We have traveled together through the ups and downs of self-rediscovery in building a relationship with yourself, and now it is time to take a moment to look back and see how far you have come. Reflection is not just about remembering what you have learned; it is about truly understanding it and making sure it sticks with you as you continue on your journey.

In these guided reflection exercises, you'll have the chance to revisit key moments, ideas, and lessons from the book. This is your opportunity to reinforce what you have discovered about yourself and your relationships.

Reflection helps you see your progress, recognize your growth, and identify areas where you might want to focus more attention. It is also a powerful tool for self-accountability, ensuring that you stay committed to the positive changes you have started to make.

Think of this chapter as a conversation with yourself. Be honest, be kind, and give yourself the space to fully explore your thoughts and feelings. Let's dive in and re-embrace the wonderful journey you have embarked on!

Finally, this chapter is also dedicated to encouraging you to take proactive steps in your ongoing journey of self-rediscovery and building conscious connections. Let's explore how you can continue to move forward with confidence and purpose. I want to conclude this chapter with the following encouragements.

Take proactive steps in your ongoing journey

As we almost come to the close of this book, it is important to recognize that this is not the end of your journey—it is just the beginning. You have spent time reflecting, learning, and rediscovering parts of yourself that may have been hidden or overlooked. Now, it is time to take all you have rediscovered and put it into action. You can do that in the exercises in chapters one to six if you haven't yet.

Embrace small changes

One of the most powerful ways to move forward is by embracing small, consistent changes. It is easy to feel overwhelmed by the idea of making big life changes, but remember that significant transformations often begin with small steps.

Think of it like planting a garden: you don't see the flowers bloom overnight. It takes time, care, and patience. Start by identifying one small change you can make in your daily routine that aligns with the person you want to become. Maybe it is setting aside ten minutes each morning for mindfulness, reaching out to an old friend, or simply drinking more water. These small actions build momentum and create a foundation for bigger changes down the road.

Set realistic goals

Setting goals is an essential part of moving forward, but it is crucial to set goals that are realistic and attainable. Rather than focusing on what you want to achieve in the distant future, concentrate on what you can accomplish in the near term. Break down larger goals into smaller, manageable steps. For instance, if your goal is to improve your physical health, start by committing to a 15-minute walk each day. As you achieve these smaller goals, you'll build confidence and motivation to tackle larger challenges.

Stay connected

Building and maintaining conscious connections is a key theme throughout this book, and it is something that will continue to be important as you move forward. Reach out to those around you—friends, family, colleagues—and nurture those relationships. Don't be afraid to show vulnerability and share your journey with others. Authentic connections are built on honesty and openness. Surround yourself with people who uplift and support you, and don't hesitate to distance yourself from those who drain your energy or bring negativity into your life.

Practice self-compassion

As you take proactive steps forward, it is inevitable that you'll encounter setbacks and challenges. It is important to practice self-compassion during these times. Be kind to yourself and recognize that making mistakes is a natural part of growth. Instead of being overly critical, ask yourself what you can learn from the experience and how you can use that knowledge to move forward.

Remember, self-compassion is not about letting yourself off the hook; it is about acknowledging your humanity and treating yourself with the same kindness you would offer a friend.

Keep learning

The journey of self-rediscovery is a lifelong process, and there is always something new to learn. Stay curious and open-minded. Seek out new experiences, read books, take courses, and engage in conversations that challenge your perspectives. Learning keeps you adaptable and helps you grow in ways you might not have anticipated. Make a habit of reflecting on what you learn and how it can be applied to your life.

Create a vision

Having a clear vision of where you want to go can provide direction and motivation. Take some time to imagine your ideal future. What does it look like? How do you feel? What are you doing? Write down your vision and keep it somewhere visible. This vision is not set in stone; it is a living, breathing guide that can evolve as you do. Use it as a source of inspiration and a reminder of why you are taking these proactive steps.

Celebrate your progress

It is easy to get caught up in the hustle of moving forward and forget to celebrate how far you have come. Make it a habit to acknowledge and celebrate your progress, no matter how small it may seem. Reflect on the positive changes you have made and the goals you have achieved. Celebrating your wins reinforces positive behavior and keeps you motivated to continue on your journey.

Take care of your well-being

Your physical, emotional, and mental well-being are the foundation of your journey. Make self-care a priority. This means getting enough sleep, eating nutritious foods, exercising regularly, and taking time to relax and recharge. Pay attention to your emotional health by practicing mindfulness, journaling, or talking to a trusted friend or therapist. When you take care of yourself, you are better equipped to handle challenges and make meaningful progress.

Be patient

Change takes time, and it is important to be patient with yourself. There will be moments of frustration and doubt, but remember that every step forward, no matter how small, is progress. Trust the process and give yourself the grace to grow at your own pace. Keep in mind that the journey of self-rediscovery is unique to each individual. Your path does not have to look like anyone else's.

Stay committed

Finally, stay committed to your journey. There will be ups and downs, but perseverance is key. Keep reminding yourself of your why—why you started this journey and what you hope to achieve. Surround yourself with positive influences, and don't be afraid to seek help or guidance when needed. Stay focused on your vision and trust that every step you take brings you closer to the person you want to become.

Moving forward is an ongoing process, filled with opportunities for growth and connection. By taking proactive steps, staying connected, practicing self-compassion, and remaining committed to your journey, you can continue to build a fulfilling and conscious life. Remember, you have the power to shape your future. Embrace the journey, celebrate your progress, and keep moving forward with confidence and purpose.

To conclude this chapter, I want to share examples of some **core values explained, with practical everyday situations and how to set boundaries.**

Core value	Explanation	Everyday situation	Setting Boundaries
Integrity	Upholding honesty and moral principles	Submitting an accurate expense report at work	Clearly communicate expectations about truthfulness in reporting. Implement consequences for dishonesty
Respect	Treating others with consideration and dignity	Active listening during a disagreement	Establish guidelines for respectful communication. Address disrespectful behavior promptly with consequences
Responsibility	Being accountable for one's actions and commitments	Meeting deadlines on work projects	Clearly define expectations and deadlines. Address repeated failure to meet responsibilities with constructive feedback and consequences

Core value	Explanation	Everyday situation	Setting Boundaries
Empathy	Understanding and sharing others' feelings	Supporting a friend going through a tough time	Encourage open communication about emotional needs. Respect personal space but be available for support when needed
Teamwork	Collaborating effectively with others toward a common goal	Group project at school or work	Clearly define individual roles and expectations. Address issues of uncooperative behavior with constructive feedback
Excellence	Striving for the highest quality in everything	Delivering a polished presentation	Establish a standard of excellence. Provide constructive criticism for subpar work and encourage improvement
Accountability	Taking ownership of one's actions and decisions	Admitting and rectifying a mistake at work	Foster an environment where mistakes are acknowledged without fear. Address repeated lack of accountability with appropriate consequences

Core value	Explanation	Everyday situation	Setting Boundaries
Gratitude	Recognizing and appreciating the positive aspects of life	Expressing thanks for a colleague's help	Encourage a culture of gratitude. Set limits on negativity and encourage positive communication
Courage	Facing challenges and adversity with bravery	Speaking up against injustice in the workplace	Establish a safe environment for expressing concerns. Address any retaliation promptly and decisively
Flexibility	Adapting to change and willingness to compromise	Adjusting to unexpected changes in project plans	Communicate expectations for flexibility. Establish limits on the extent to which individuals are expected to adapt without proper communication and consideration
Family	Family represents the core social unit and often serves as a source of love, support, and belonging. It includes immediate relatives like parents and siblings and can extend to close	A typical everyday situation reflecting the value of family might be gathering for a weekly family dinner. This is a time for everyone to share their experiences, offer support, and	Setting boundaries with family involves maintaining a balance between being supportive and respecting individual needs for space and autonomy. For instance, it is important to

Core value	Explanation	Everyday situation	Setting Boundaries
	friends and other significant relationships. The concept of family is central to personal identity and emotional well-being	strengthen their bonds	communicate clearly about personal time and responsibilities, ensuring everyone understands and respects that
Quality time	Quality time refers to spending meaningful and focused time with loved ones, engaging in activities that strengthen relationships and create lasting memories. It emphasizes presence and attentiveness rather than the duration of time spent together	An everyday situation for quality time might be a parent and child playing a game or reading a book together without distractions. This uninterrupted interaction helps build a deeper connection and fosters positive relationships	To prioritize quality time, it is crucial to set boundaries around work and digital devices. For example, establishing "*no phone*" zones during meals or designating certain hours for family activities can help ensure that time spent together is meaningful and undistracted
Balance	Balance is the equilibrium between various aspects of life, such as work, family, personal time, and health. Achieving balance means ensuring that no single area is	An everyday situation illustrating balance might be an individual managing their day by allocating specific times for work, exercise, family, and personal hobbies.	Setting boundaries to maintain balance involves prioritizing and scheduling time for different activities. This might include setting strict work hours, making

Core value	Explanation	Everyday situation	Setting Boundaries
	disproportionately neglected or overemphasized, leading to a more fulfilling and less stressful life	This approach ensures that all important areas receive adequate attention	time for regular exercise, and planning social activities. For instance, a person might set a rule to not check work emails after 7 PM, ensuring evenings are reserved for relaxation and family time
Self-Care	Self-care refers to the deliberate activities and practices individuals engage in to maintain their physical, mental, and emotional well-being. It is about recognizing one's needs and taking steps to ensure they are met, promoting overall health, and preventing burnout	A busy professional schedules regular breaks throughout their workday to take short walks, practice mindfulness, and eat nutritious meals. This helps them manage stress and maintain focus and productivity	An individual might decline an invitation to a social event because they recognize the need for a restful evening at home. By saying no, they prioritize their well-being and avoid overextending themselves
Compassion	Compassion involves empathy and concern for the suffering of others, accompanied by a desire to help	A coworker notices a colleague seems stressed and overwhelmed with a project. They offer to help with some tasks or	While showing compassion, it is important to avoid taking on others' burdens to the detriment of one's well-being.

Core value	Explanation	Everyday situation	Setting Boundaries
	alleviate that suffering. It is about recognizing the shared human experience and responding with kindness and understanding	simply lend a listening ear, showing understanding and support	For instance, someone might offer emotional support to a friend going through a tough time but also communicate their own need for space to recharge
Authenticity	Authenticity involves being true to oneself and expressing one's genuine thoughts, feelings, and values. It means acting in alignment with one's true self rather than conforming to external expectations or pressures	An employee provides honest feedback in a team meeting about a project's direction, even though their opinion might differ from the majority. They value integrity and believe their perspective is important for the team's success	A person may choose to leave a job that conflicts with their personal values, even if it means facing uncertainty. By doing so, they maintain their integrity and stay true to their authentic self

9. Coming Home to Yourself

Welcome to the final chapter of *Re-Embrace You! A Journey of Self-Rediscovery to Building Conscious Connection*. As I close the book with this final chapter, it is important to pause and reflect on the profound journey we have embarked upon together. This is not just the culmination of a book; it is the beginning of a deeper, more meaningful engagement with ourselves and the world around us.

I want to encourage you to:

Keep Growing, Keep Connecting

Now that we have journeyed through the pages of self-rediscovery and learned the importance of conscious connections, you might be wondering, "What is next?" The truth is, the journey does not end here. The road to self-awareness and building deeper relationships is ongoing—there is always more to explore, more to understand, and more to improve.

Stay Curious About Yourself

Curiosity didn't just kill the cat; it also built the castle. Staying curious about who you are and who you can become is vital. Remember, every day is a new chance to learn something about yourself. Whether it is uncovering a hidden talent, understanding a deep-seated fear, or simply recognizing what makes you happy or sad, each discovery adds another layer to your understanding of yourself.

Try keeping a journal of your thoughts and feelings. Not only will it help you track your growth, but it will also serve as a reflection of your changing inner landscape. As you write, ask yourself questions like,

"What brought me joy today?" or "What challenged my values?" Use your answers not just to learn but to reshape your approach to similar situations in the future.

Nurture Your Relationships

Just as you evolve, so do your relationships. Each person in your life offers a unique mirror, reflecting parts of you that you may not always see. Engage deeply with the people around you. Listen to understand, not just to respond. Show appreciation, not just for what they do, but for who they are.

Remember to schedule regular check-ins with close friends and family. These don't have to be formal—sometimes a quick call or a coffee date is all it takes to reconnect. During these times, make it a point to discuss more than just day-to-day activities; dive into your hopes, fears, dreams, and disappointments. These conversations not only strengthen bonds but also promote mutual growth.

Embrace New Connections

Stepping out of your comfort zone can be daunting, but it is also where growth thrives. Be open to forming new relationships. Each new connection offers a fresh perspective and possibly a new friend. Attend community events, join clubs or groups that align with your interests, or simply reach out to someone you have wanted to get to know better.

As you meet new people, bring into play the lessons you have learned about values and boundaries. These will help you quickly see who resonates with your true self and who might be better as just an acquaintance. Not every person needs to become a close friend, but every interaction is an opportunity to learn and grow.

Reflect and Adjust

As you continue on your journey, regularly take the time to reflect on both yourself and your relationships. Are you living in alignment with your values? Are your relationships supportive and balanced? Reflection is the compass that keeps you on your path, ensuring that you are moving in the direction you want to go.

If something feels off, don't be afraid to adjust. Change can be refreshing and necessary. It might mean setting new boundaries, spending more time alone, or even parting ways with someone who no longer fits the life you aspire to live. Remember, it is okay to outgrow relationships just as it is okay to outgrow old versions of yourself.

The journey of self-rediscovery and building conscious connections is a beautiful, endless cycle of learning, growing, and evolving. Keep moving, keep discovering, and keep embracing every part of this incredible adventure. The more you invest in understanding and nurturing your relationships—with yourself and others—the richer your life will become. Here is to continuing your journey with courage, curiosity, and an open heart.

Write a letter to your future self

Reflect on your commitment to embracing your true self, based on your core values and setting healthy boundaries, and use these aspects as guidance to build conscious connections with others. This is my letter to my future self!

Dear Future Me,

Hey there! It is me from the past, writing to remind you of some important things.
Right now, I am on a journey to fully embrace who I am, and

I want to check in with you to see how things are going.

First off, I hope you are staying true to your core values. Remember how we spent time figuring out what truly matters to us? We have worked hard to define our core values - Fidelity, Compassion, and Empowerment were at the top of our list. I hope you are still living by those principles. These values are like our North Star, they guide us in making the right choices, even when it is tough. Are you still making decisions that align with these values? They keep us grounded and help us stay true to who we are.

Setting boundaries was a big step for us. It was not easy learning to say no without feeling guilty. But we learned that our time and energy are precious, and it is okay to protect them. Are you still practicing this? It is okay to put yourself first sometimes; you can't pour from an empty cup.

Remember, it is not about shutting people out; it is about creating space for what truly matters and for the people who uplift us. Speaking of people, building conscious connections has been such a rewarding part of this journey. We have focused on surrounding ourselves with those who respect our boundaries and share our values. How's that going? Have you met new friends who inspire you and support your growth? Are you nurturing the relationships that bring joy and meaning to your life?

Don't forget to check in with yourself regularly. Are you still journaling, meditating, or doing whatever helps you stay grounded? Self-reflection is key to staying aligned with our true self.

Lastly, be kind to yourself.

There will be times when we slip up or face challenges. That is okay.
Embrace those moments as opportunities to learn and grow.
You have come so far, and I am proud of you for that.

Keep shining and stay true to who you are. The journey is not always easy, but it is worth it.

With love and hope,
Your Past Self

Embracing ourselves fully does not mean we have reached a state of perfection; rather, it is about accepting our imperfections and turning them into sources of strength. It is about standing firmly within our crafted boundaries and respecting those of others, which enables us to form healthier, more conscious connections.

Through the chapters, we have navigated the complex landscapes of self-awareness, vulnerability, core values, and boundaries. Each section was not just a topic, but a step forward on a path back to our true selves. Like pieces of a puzzle, they have come together to form a clearer picture of who we are and who we aspire to be.

Remember the early days of this journey? It is about unlearning as much as it is about learning anew. Through exercises and reflections, we have not only rediscovered facets of our identity but have begun to reshape them with intention and grace. Continue exploring and nurturing their relationships with themselves and others.

As I reflect on the process of writing this book, I am struck by how my own journey mirrored the one I was describing. There were moments of doubt and frustration, times when the right words seemed just out of reach. Yet, there was also immense growth and understanding gained through each faced challenge. This book, in many ways, was my own re-embrace, a testament to the transformative power of returning to myself. A very dear friend of mine, Jose Parami, remarked on an author's journey with this quote: ***"Writing heals the writer and uplifts the reader."*** This quote only stresses what I mentioned earlier in this paragraph.

As you move forward, carry with you the knowledge that rediscovering yourself is an ongoing process. Life will change, as will you. The values and boundaries you have set may evolve, and that is okay. What is crucial is that you remain true to your journey, conscious of your growth, and open to the infinite possibilities that embracing your authentic self brings.

In this final chapter, I urge you not to view this as an end but a vibrant new beginning. Let the insights from this book be your guide, your reminder, and your inspiration as you continue to build and rebuild the most important relationship you have—the one with yourself.

Thank you for allowing me to be a part of your journey. I hope that you will enjoy this book as much as I have enjoyed writing it!

As we part ways on this chapter, remember: *the path to self-rediscovery does not end here*. It is a beautiful, perpetual journey of coming home to ourselves, time and time again.

Here is to embracing ourselves, today, tomorrow, and every day after.
Let's walk forward together, re-embraced and renewed.

Are you ready to start your journey of self re-discovery and transformation?

Re-embrace You is more than just a book—it's a guide to unlocking your true potential and building meaningful connections. This book offers the tools, insights, and inspiration you need to unlock the wisdom, tools, and inspiration you need to embrace your true self and create a life filled with purpose and joy.

Click "Buy Now" to begin your journey towards self-love, growth, and conscious connection.

Let's connect on:

https://leadership-refocused.com/home
https://www.linkedin.com/in/marlene-gravenberch-5655a61a
https://www.facebook.com/LeadershipRefocused
https://www.facebook.com/MMIGravenberch
https://www.instagram.com/marlenegravenberch

About the Author

Hi, I'm Marlène Gravenberch

In my personal life, I am a mom of two adults (lady and gent) who have given me four beautiful grandkids, making me a grandma. I am blessed with a huge family of brothers and sisters and intimate friends who became family too: cheering one another, laughing together, and crying together. Since I was born and raised in Suriname (South America) with a vibrant and diverse culture because of our history, I am a cultural admirer.

In my professional life, I am an empowerment advocate, in the role of personal and professional development coach and conservation enthusiast with over thirty years of experience in a variety of industries with over three decades of diverse experience across different industries. This led to the founding of Leadership Refocused.

I have been an educator and HR Manager for years, till June 2023. For the past 3 years, I have been coaching individuals in their personal and professional development, of which many of them are women.

In July 2023, I started my own coaching business. I am dedicated to empowering leaders, with a bigger focus on women.

Looking back, I come to realize that I always had that coaching DNA within me, knowing at an early age what I wanted to become – a teacher -. Looking back, educating and empowering others has been the common thread in my life.

Becoming a teacher has set the tone for my mission, which is igniting possibilities, cultivating excellence, creating inclusive and empowering environments that unlock the full (leadership) potential within each person, and empowering their journey toward success, especially women.

During that journey, I also discovered that first and foremost developing a relationship with yourself first, will help you develop and foster a healthy relationship with yourself and others. Those are the reasons for writing this book.

My passion for research and my curiosity, have resulted in me co-authoring: *Customer Centricity and Innovation in Automotive Sales* (with Dr. Galill William, 2017) & *Mentorship And Professional Growth For Conservationists In Primate-Range Countries* (with Sylvia Atsalis, PhD - https://doi.org/10.1002/ajp.23592.

Together with other coaches, I have hosted a workshop titled *Reinvent Yourself; Reset to Evolve*! on April 28, 2024. I have been a two-time guest on a radio program *Van Hier Naar Beter* with Shanine Dwaalster. *(Starting Here to Become a Better Version of Yourself)*. I was also a guest (March 2024) in a podcast from Marissa Warren *Elevate*, where I highlighted the topic of *The importance of developing a relationship with yourself first*.

I have had my share of struggles, from entering the male-dominated work environment and being -most of the time- the only woman in the management team. Experiencing just being tolerated by male colleagues and in a specific case, one of my male colleagues openly expressed his dislike, only because I wanted to mediate between him and the CEO, in my role as HR Manager.

In my personal life, I struggled to hold on to a relationship for almost 30 years, trying to fix me and my partner, while I was getting more broken.

In 2013, I came to the crossroads, where I told myself to make a decision that would bring me peace. This journey is for another book! ☺

Hadn't it been for my growth path, I would not have been able to deal healthily with these challenges.

Today, when Marlène is not enjoying family time, sipping wine with close friends, enjoying nature, reading books, or listening to different genres of music, you'll often find her helping as a volunteer. Now she is an active member on the board of The Prasoro Foundation (a Home for children in need), Coaching young adults in different areas of their interest and coaching/mentoring students in thesis writing. As part of giving back, I also offer free coaching sessions to women who cannot afford it.

For further insights into Marlène and the ways she can support you in personal and professional development, explore her expertise at

https://leadership-refocused.com
https://www.facebook.com/MMIGravenberch
https://www.instagram.com/marlenegravenberch
https://www.linkedin.com/in/marlene-gravenberch-5655a61a
https://www.facebook.com/LeadershipRefocused

Made in the USA
Monee, IL
20 December 2024

74850947R00059